JOHN RUTTER

Variations on an Easter theme

This work was given its first performance by Ray and Beth Chenault in Washington National Cathedral, USA, on 31 July 1983.

Duration 6½ minutes

for Ray and Beth Chenault

VARIATIONS ON AN EASTER THEME

(O Filii et Filiae)

JOHN RUTTER

poco allargando

Slow (♩ = 60-66) *with slight rubato*

Solo stop 1

mp

Sw. *p*

Ped.

12

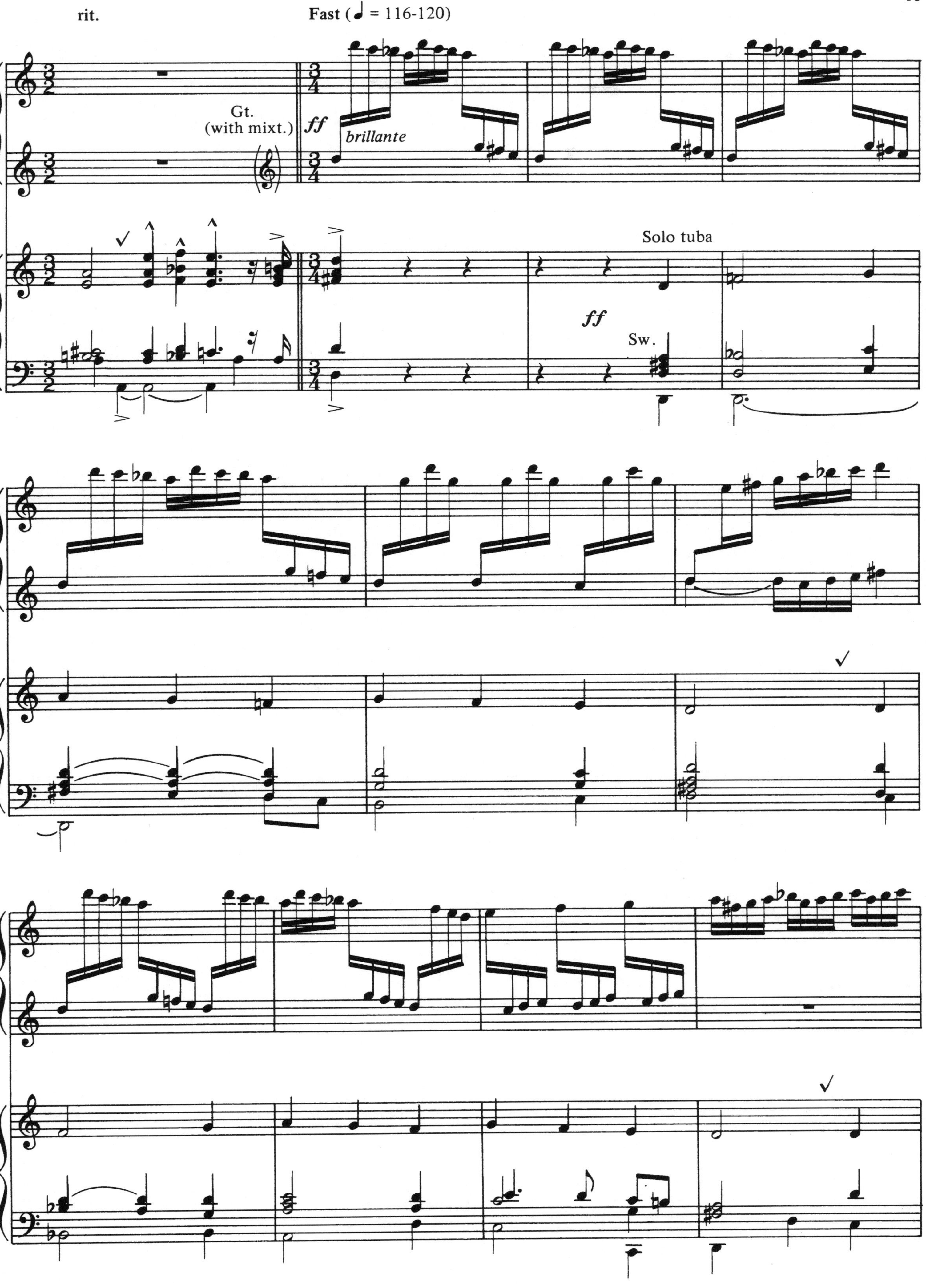
rit.
Fast (♩ = 116-120)
Gt.
(with mixt.)
ff
brillante
Solo tuba
ff
Sw.

Largamente

Sw.

Tuba

Printed by Caligraving Limited Thetford Norfolk England